Dear Readers & Educators,

It is a big galaxy out there. Even though you can't ride a bicycle to the moon or any other planet, you do have a role in the galaxy and on this small blue planet.

Our role as humans is to explore, to learn, and to pass on what we know.

The "You Can't" series asks readers to let curiosity, reading, research, and thinking lead to all the possibilities of what we *can* do and be as humans.

We would love to know what you have learned from these titles and how you have used it to inspire learning in others.

Visit the "Educators & Librarians" page at **www.blueapplebooks.com** for curriculum and to share your teaching ideas.

Other Titles in This Series:

You Can't Taste a Pickle with Your Ear
You Can't See Your Bones with Binoculars
You Can't Take Your Body to a Car Mechanic
You Can't Build a House If You're a Hippo
You Can't Spot a Duck in the Desert
You Can't Use Your Brain If You're a Jellyfish
You Can't See a Dodo at the Zoo
You Can't Lay an Egg If You're an Elephant

You Can't RIDE A BICYCLE TO THE MOON!

A Book About SPACE TRAVEL

Harriet Ziefert

pictures by Amanda Haley

BLUE APPLE

To Charlie and Lucy
—H.Z.

To Melissa and Luna with love
—A.H.

Text copyright © 2014 by Harriet Ziefert
Illustrations copyright © 2014 by Amanda Haley

J. Patrick Lewis, "First Men on the Moon" from *A Burst of Firsts:
Doers, Shakers, and Record Breakers*, published by The Dial Press.
Copyright © 2001 by J. Patrick Lewis.
Reprinted by permission of Curtis Brown, Ltd.

Published in the United States 2014 by
 Blue Apple Books
515 Valley Street, Maplewood, N J 07040
www.blueapplebooks.com

First Edition
Printed in China
ISBN: 978-1-60905-419-9

1 3 5 7 9 10 8 6 4 2

Contents

WITHDRAWN

INTRODUCTION

Hey diddle diddle,
The cat and the fiddle,
The cow jumped over the moon;
The little dog laughed
To see such a sight,
And the dish ran away
with the spoon.

This poem has been around for at least 300 years. For thousands of years, there have been stories, poems, and pictures imagining what it might be like on the moon.

Are there people, or gods, or aliens, or monsters up there—or nothing at all?

We just had to find out!

How big is the moon?

The earth is four times as big as the moon.

What shape is the moon?

The moon is round like a ball,
but it doesn't always look that way to us.

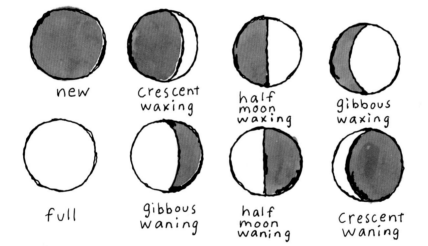

new   crescent waxing   half moon waxing   gibbous waxing

full   gibbous waning   half moon waning   crescent waning

During the 27 days it takes for the moon to travel around the earth, only certain parts of it are lit up. From earth, we see it as a full circle that gets whittled down to a skinny crescent— and then it fills out again.

A full moon may look golden, reddish, orange, or bright white.

"Only once in a blue moon" is an expression referring to something that doesn't happen very often.

What's the moon made of?

A silly idea people once had: cheese! In fact, the moon
is mostly rocky. It has craters, mountains, and valleys.
Water, not cheese, was discovered on the moon in 2009.

What's the weather on the moon?

The moon is surrounded by a thin layer of gases.
It's never windy on the moon, but the moon does have
a range of temperatures.

A person could be totally frozen on the moon. Or burn up.
YIKES!

How old is the moon?

1.5 billion years old. The earth is 4.5 billion years old.

Is there a Man in the Moon?

Just like clouds look like certain
objects, some people think
they can see the profile of a
man's face on the moon's surface.
This is because there are dark
patches (which are really craters)
on the lunar surface.
Do you see a face in this photo?

What lights up the moon?

Half of the moon is always dark. The other half reflects
the sunlight shining on it. If there were no sun,
we would not be able to see the moon.

Does the moon move?

Constantly! The moon travels around the earth in a circle,
called an orbit. It takes the moon about a month
to travel around the earth . . .

27 days, 7 hours, 43 minutes, 11.6 seconds to be exact!

How close is the moon?

It is 250,000 miles away from earth.
Here's how long a trip would take:

• by car (at 55 mph): 130 days

• by rocket (at 36,000 mph): 8 hours, 35 minutes

• at the speed of light: 1.52 seconds

How long would it take by bicycle?
Sorry, you can't ride a bicycle to the moon!

Biking to the Moon

I won't be home for dinner.
I'm biking to the moon!

I won't need an umbrella.
I'm biking to the moon!

I won't need a cell phone.
I'm biking to the moon!

I won't wear a windbreaker.
I'm biking to the moon!

So...

What WILL I need
For a bike trip to the moon?
A little kit for bike repair
And lots, and lots, and LOTS—
of AIR!

Humans have driven special lunar rover vehicles, walked, jumped around, planted flags, and hit a golf ball on the moon.

How did they get there? You're about to find out!

Chapter 1: Me, first! The Space Race

1959

American and Soviet scientists wanted to be the first to land an unmanned spacecraft on the moon. The Soviets won this part of the "space race."

Actually, the Soviets' Luna-2 didn't land so much as crash-and-smash onto the moon. Luckily, no one was on board!

Dog-stronauts

The first animals in space were 57 Soviet female dogs. Some traveled there alone; some went in pairs.

In 1959, two dogs and a rabbit named Little Martha traveled into space.

1960

In 1960, the spacecraft carrying the dogs Shutka and Comet crash-landed in freezing-cold Siberia—2,200 miles from where it had launched. Four days later, the dogs were found—very cold and tired, but alive.

The hero-dogs regained their health, and Comet later had a litter of puppies. Behold the power of the pooch!

Monkey Missions

The first passengers in the American space program included monkeys, chimps, and mice. Patricia and Mike, a pair of monkeys, rode with two mice named Mildred and Albert on a flight in 1952. They helped scientists learn more about weightlessness and what it might be like for people to travel at a speed of 2,000 miles per hour.

First in Space?

Brave One, Little Comet,
Gypsy, Leika, Starlet,
Albina, Shutka, Pearl.
57 space pioneers,
and every one—a girl!

Were humans first in space?
Is that what you thought?
Oh no, nuh-uh, not true!
The first were dog-Stronauts!

First People in Space

1961

Yuri Gagarin, a 27-year-old Soviet astronaut, became the first man to travel into space.

Gagarin's spacecraft (Vostok 1) completed one orbit of the earth and landed 108 minutes after take-off.

Using a parachute, Gagarin escaped from his spaceship before it crash-landed. But Gagarin never worried about the landing— he just wanted to make sure that he had enough sausages to snack on during his post-flight trip home!

1963

Another Soviet, 26-year-old Valentina Tereshkova, was the first woman in space.

1st Woman in Space

Valentina Tereshkova

Before she became an astronaut, Valentina took skydiving lessons and worked in a factory that made cloth. Her mission took almost three days, and she orbited the earth 48 times.

A crater on the far side of the moon is named after her.

Robot-tronaut?

1966

NASA, America's National Aeronautics and Space Administration, sent a robot-controlled spaceship to make sure it was possible to land safely on the moon. The Surveyor 1 made a perfect, "soft" landing.

Now that we knew we could go that far and land without crashing… it was time!

A giant leap for mankind!

1969

On July 20, 1969, millions watched their TVs to see Neil Armstrong, Buzz Aldrin, and their pilot, Michael Collins, land on the moon.

Amazing! Or, as Commander Armstrong put it as he became the first person to step onto the moon's surface:

"That's one small step for man, one giant leap for mankind."

Suiting Up

Each astronaut's space suit had 22 layers of fabric that were glued, taped, and sewn together. Since they didn't know for sure what being on the moon would be like, they had to guess at some of what would be needed to protect the astronauts and make it possible for them to function during Apollo 11's eight-day mission.

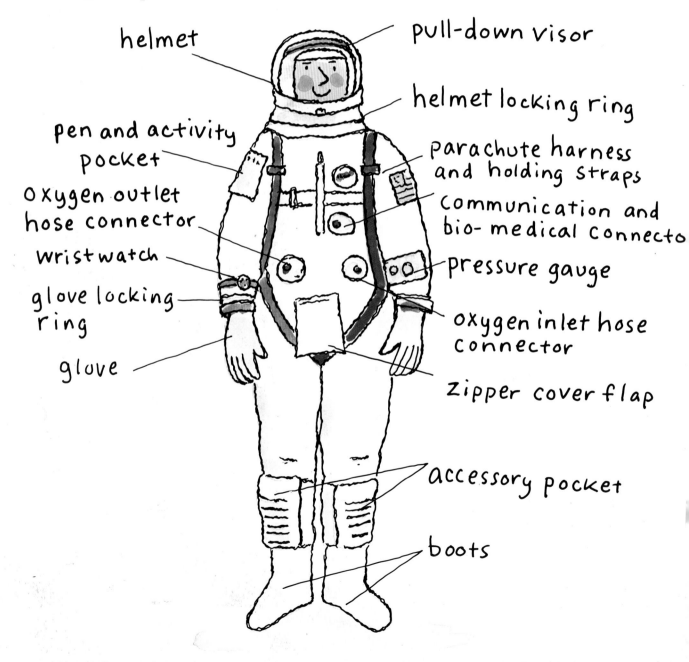

helmet

pull-down visor

helmet locking ring

pen and activity pocket

parachute harness and holding straps

oxygen outlet hose connector

communication and bio-medical connecto

wristwatch

pressure gauge

glove locking ring

oxygen inlet hose connector

glove

zipper cover flap

accessory pocket

boots

First Men on the Moon

That afternoon in mid-July,
Two pilgrims watched from distant space
The moon ballooning in the sky.
They rose to meet it face-to-face.

Their spidery spaceship, Eagle, dropped
Down gently on the lunar sand.
And when the module's engines stopped,
Rapt silence fell across the land.

The first man down the ladder, Neil,
Spoke words that we remember now—
"One small step…" It made us feel
As if we were there too, somehow.

When Neil planted the flag and Buzz
Collected lunar rocks and dust,
They hopped like kangaroos because
Of gravity. Or wanderlust?

A quarter million miles away,
One small blue planet watched in awe.
And no one who was there that day
Will soon forget the sight they saw.

— by J. Patrick Lewis

Dangerous Missions

1970

BANG! On April 13, 1970, that's what the astronauts on the Apollo 13 mission heard when electrical wiring caused an explosion.

Alarm lights flashed. The spaceship shook.

The crew wouldn't be able to land on the moon—but would they be able to get home safely?

They had to shut down heating and cooling systems, and stretch out their water supply. NASA's ground crew sent instructions to help the astronauts handle the cold conditions and to fix the spacecraft.

On April 17th, the space capsule splashed down in the Pacific Ocean. Phew!

What the NASA astronauts, scientists, and engineers learned from the Apollo 13 mission would help make future space flights safer.

What do you need most when traveling in the galaxy? Training, skill, courage, And in-gen-u-ity!

Chapter 2:
The Craft of Spacecraft

It takes education, hard work, imagination, and a spirit of adventure to figure out how to build things that can travel into space.

Think about how many parts there are on a simple bicycle. Then imagine how hard it must have been to build a vehicle to travel in space.

Here's what some of the first bicycles looked like:

Hot air balloons, airplanes, helicopters, and spacecraft show how much people want to fly into the sky—and beyond!

Satellites

The first spacecraft were satellites, manmade objects launched into space to orbit the earth.

The first satellites helped us know what materials could handle a trip to space. Later, they were equipped with telescopes and other equipment that help us collect information about our galaxy.

Satellites take pictures, make our cell phones work, enable television signals, let us know where things are and what's happening with the weather.

Over 5,000 satellites have been launched into space. Most travel within three orbits around the earth or sun.

Oh no, oh no!
Which way do I go?
Big city, small town—
Wherever you may roam—
A GPS satellite
Will help you get back home.

Spaceships

Shuttles, modules, and rocket ships are all types of spacecraft that were made to carry passengers into space and return them back to earth.

Before they could do that, rockets needed to be invented, along with fuel to power the rockets!

Thousands, maybe millions, of people over hundreds of years have worked to create and discover the technology, materials, and systems that make it possible to zoom to the moon.

Food, toilets, beds, clothing, and ways to keep clean all had to be re-imagined so that they could fit the conditions inside the spacecraft.

The Lunar Rover

Neil Armstrong and Buzz Aldrin walked and did what they called "the kangaroo jump" on the moon.

Later on, an electric car called the Lunar Roving Vehicle (LRV) was invented.

Driving to the Moon?

Well, not exactly. But people needed to figure out how to get the Lunar Rover to fit inside a space shuttle. The solution: a hinge that helped it fold in half! When all folded up, it is just a little bigger than a washing machine.

Driving on the Moon

Yes, it does do that!

The LRV moves at about 8 mph. The people who created it figured out how to keep it from floating away.

The LRV allowed astronauts to explore much more of the moon than they could have on foot.

There haven't been any lunar car crashes, but one LRV did get damaged, and the astronauts had to use a map as a makeshift fender.

Crater Races

Moon Rover, Moon Rover,
Won't you come over
And take me someplace cool to play?
We'll explore Humorum, Crisium, Vaporum—
And race across craters all day!

Chapter 3
Living in Space

In June 1983, Sally Ride blasted off with four other astronauts on the spaceship Challenger. She was the first American female astronaut.

The group circled around the earth for seven days.

Sally Ride

Why does an astronaut wear special clothes?

Astronauts wear special clothes to protect themselves from the conditions in outer space.

A space suit can warm you up, cool you off, and give you air to breath. It can even have a built-in toilet!

A suit that has a rocket-powered backpack makes it possible for an astronaut to fly around in space.

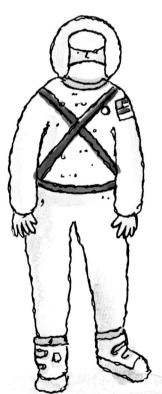

Here's what Sally Ride wore on her space voyage.

In my Space Suit I Suppose There's no Way To Scratch my nose!

In her book, *To Space and Back*, Sally Ride describes what it was like to travel, eat, sleep, go to the bathroom, make a peanut butter sandwich, and do experiments in space.

Weightlessness

Sally had this to say:

"All adventures — especially into new territory — are scary and there has always been an element of danger in space travel."
— Sally Ride

"The best part of being in space is being weightless. It feels wonderful to float; to be upside down as often as I'm right side up!"

How do astronauts eat?

A food game played in space, but not in your kitchen!—

An astronaut throws a cookie into the air. Another astronaut, floating along, tries to catch it in his or her mouth!

"Food trays are strapped to our legs. Most food is sticky so it stays on a spoon. Sometimes a blob of pudding escapes and we have to catch it before it splatters on a wall."
— Sally Ride

The first space meals were a lot like baby food packed into toothpaste-like tubes. The astronauts squeezed the goopy foods into their mouths. American astronauts ate applesauce. Soviet astronauts liked a vegetable soup called borscht.

For flavored drinks, water is added to powdered mixes. Orange-flavored Tang was once a very popular drink on both earth and in outer space.

How many astronauts does it take to make a peanut butter sandwich?

At least two! One has to hold the lid and jar of peanut butter, while another holds the knife and the bread.

What should I eat in space today?
Something that won't float away!
Food that sticks onto a spoon
Is best when dining on the moon!

**How does an astronaut
go to the bathroom?**

While traveling in the galaxy,
Astronauts must poop and pee.
An astronaut's toilet goal?
Stay attached to the toilet bowl!

"To use the toilet,
I sit on the seat, use
the leg restraints to
keep myself from
floating away, turn on
the air suction, and
the waste is pulled
into the bowl."
— Sally Ride

How does an astronaut sleep?

It is surprisingly easy to get comfortable and sleep in space.

Some sleep while freely floating, just crossing their arms and legs, and maybe wearing a mask over their eyes. Other astronauts attach a sleeping bag to a hook, so they won't float around while they're resting.

"When I'm in orbit it seems as though I don't need as much sleep as I do on Earth. Maybe it's because I'm so excited to be in space and don't want to waste time sleeping."
— Sally Ride

When I sleep in space,
I hold my pillow tight.
If I let go of it,
I'll be chasing it all night!

At the Speed of Light

I thought I bought a ticket
To travel to the moon.
"Don't worry, Mom and Dad," I said,
"I'll be home by first of June."

But when I got on board
And buckled up for flight
I found that I was bound for Mars
Traveling at the speed of light.

And so I sent a message saying:

"I'll be home tonight!"

NOTE: Traveling at the speed of light, it would only take about four minutes to go from Earth to Mars!

Chapter 4
Tourists in Space

So far, most of the people who have traveled into space have been scientists, astronauts, and other aerospace professionals.

In the near future, people who simply want to see what it's like in space may be able to take a space vacation.

The Commercial Spaceflight Federation, Space Adventures, and Virgin Galactic are among the companies that are working to offer ordinary people a chance to visit space.

At first, it will be very expensive to buy a ticket. Space Adventures brought three citizens to visit the International Space Station. The tickets cost $20 million per person!

Celebrities and some rich folks have booked tickets for future flights. As time goes on, the ticket price will go down. But it will still cost more than a bike ride!

Housing Modules in Space

Since the 1970s, companies have been coming up with ideas for places people could stay while in space. A shuttle would take these "cabins" or "habitat modules" into space. Some of them were designed to hold as many as 74 passengers. Right now these space hotels are still a dream. But someday soon…maybe you will be checking into Motel Mars!

Space Trash

Space debris, space junk, space waste—all of these refer to trash floating in outer space. Old and leftover parts from satellites, space shuttles, and rockets make up some of this galactic garbage.

Things decay in space, but much more slowly than on earth. A non-working satellite called Vanguard I has been floating up in space since 1958!

Right now, there is no regularly used or agreed-upon method to collect space trash. A remote-controlled collection vehicle, using laser beams, and giant space sweepers are some of the things that are being designed to tackle this problem.

Conclusion

You can't get there on a bicycle, but if you like to travel and discover new places, maybe you'll visit space some day. Look up into the sky and imagine yourself being there.

I want to visit you someday
To see what you are like.
I'll put on boots and a moon-suit
And take a lunar hike.

Until that someday comes
When each day is at its end
I'll look outside my window
And wave to my Moon-friend.

Here's wishing you a great trip!

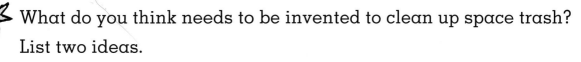

Your Destination: Space

 What do you think needs to be invented to clean up space trash? List two ideas.

 Do you think being an intergalactic garbage collector would be an interesting job? Why or why not?

 Using all you've discovered about space travel and living in space, make a list of what you would pack for your voyage to outer space.

 Think about what you did today. What are some things you did that might have been helped by satellites?

What would you do to make improvements or invent new things?

Which of these space jobs would you like to have?

space farmer	space sports inventor
space shuttle designer	space bicycle inventor
space cook	space bathroom designer
space suit maker	space rock star
space furniture maker	